Perfectly Good Muses

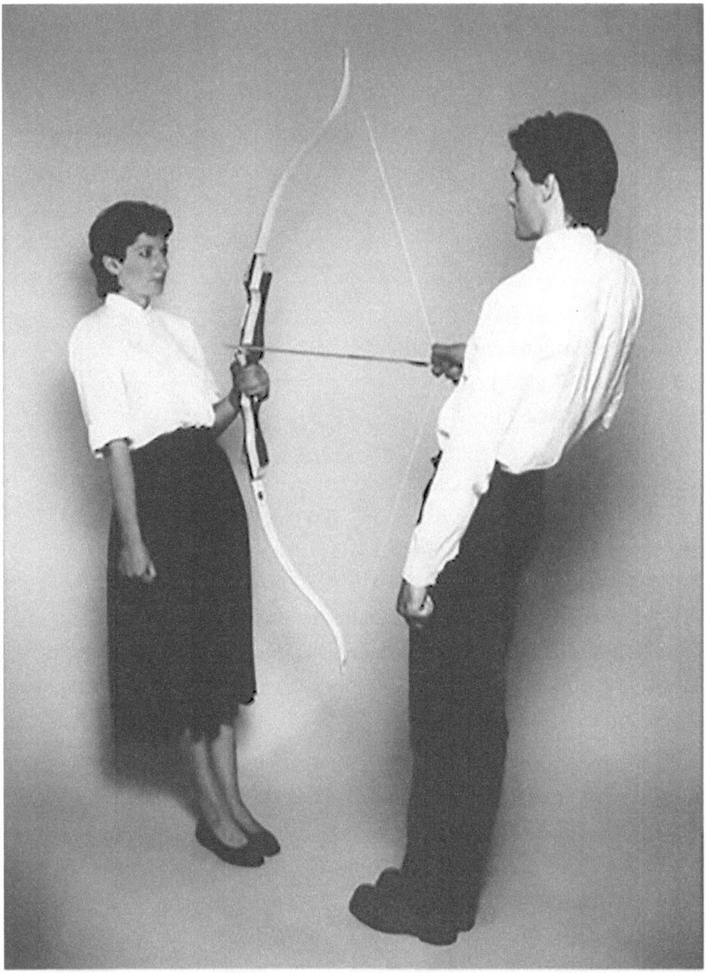

the collected apologies of Jeanette Powers

Kansas City Spartan Press Missouri

Spartan Press
Kansas City, Missouri
spartanpresskc.com

Copyright (c) Jeanette Powers, 2017
First Edition 11 7 5 3 2 1
ISBN: 978-1-946642-26-4
LCCN: 2017952568
Design, edits and layout: Jason Ryberg, Jeanette Powers
front interior photo: Marina Abramovic and Ulay "Rest Energy"
cover art and rear interior photo: Jeanette Powers

All rights reserved. No part of this publication may be reproduced or transmitted in any form or by any means, electronic or mechanical, including photocopying, recording or by info retrieval system, without prior written permission from the author.

Prospero's Books and Spartan Press would like to thank Jeanette Powers, j. d. tulloch, Jason Preu, M. Scott Douglass, Shawn Pavey, Shawn Saving, Jesse Kates, Jim Holroyd, Steven H.Bridgens, Thomas Mason, Beth Dille, Mason Wolf, The West Plaza Tomato Co., Mark McClane, the Osage Arts Community and The Robert J. Deuser Foundation For Libertarian Studies.

Next & Last by Jeanette Powers: Gasconade | NightBallet Press (Spring 2018), Beautiful Earthwoms and Abominable Stars: a tribute to Jason Ryberg, poetry split with Ezhno Martin | EMP Books (August 2017).

contact: jeanettepowers.com @novel_cliche strange.gen.et@gmail.com

TABLE OF CONTENTS

Perfectly Good Muses	/7
Silly Putty	/9
Onion	/11
Corner	/13
Eyebrow	/15
Application for a New Muse	/17
Ocean	/20
Pickle	/24
Root	/26
Parasitic Wasp	/29
Car Wreck	/31
Shaker	/33
Suburban	/35
Dragon Hoard	/38
Dream	/42
Agoraphobia	/43
Crutch	/44
Nostalgia	/46
Hokey Pokey	/48
The Muse is Present	/49

"you don't want to know how I know where you are"
--"Do You Want To" by Franz Ferdinand

PERFECTLY GOOD MUSES

I'm not on speaking terms
with a single one of my muses
and that's what keeps me writing these days.

They're still perfectly good muses
every poem is a puzzle box, a bottled ship
a sand dollar or locked vault or riddle
I'm hoping gets solved or shattered
or shared with my affections.

I'm not on speaking terms with a single one
of them, much as I love silly putty and snowglobes
much as I love pickles and whiskey and roots
much as I love musing about amused muses
but there is a line between being captivating
and being held captive.

But we did roll our eyes so good together
back in the day before we knew our worth
(before we knew our price)
back when you graced me
with your gated community flair.

It turns out the critical part of a muse lives on

in the absence of the physical part of one
muses keep renewing their lease in the mind
and I go about my business
of resuscitating life on the page.

I put a real pin in it
mount the small taxidermy
of our skin behind glass
no breath in the lungs
held still so we can see clearly.

Muses are beyond all this
this is all beneath them
and they are about
the better business of being.

SILLY PUTTY MUSE

you arrive in an egg
you are removed
you imprint on the first one you see
this is your mother

you follow her
she takes care of you
you are putty in her hands
you are impressionable

you are pressed into prints
of her choosing
a snoopy comic
charlie says: feirg doog ho

mother reforms you
and you ingest all the ink
you are pressed into
many more prints

you say !!NIW SLAYOR
you say em tnarg doG
you say drac troper
you say detivni era uoy
mother reforms you again

you lose the soft pink
supple body of being unformed
you are gray and dry with being used

silly, isn't it?

SILLY PUTTY APOLOGY

I'm sorry there's no way
to get back in the egg
that you carry those prints
with you forever now

some things
just can't be
undone

silly,
isn't it?

ONION MUSE

You are what
is at the bottom
of this crying mess
and no one can open you up
without punishment.

You are never simple.

No one really
loves an onion
it's a hard round root
best pureed
powdered
or finely diced
or maybe cubed
but the bigger the slice
of you, the more likely
left on the edge
of the plate
and you feel how thin
you must be spread
to be palatable.

There is no way

to hold more than
a half dozen onions
in one's hands.
Every attempt to embrace
one ends up with a thunk
thunk
thunk and rolls away.
The onion is combative
anyway, those noxious
fumes payback for being dug up.

Now that we are older
you see we both
don't wrinkle or budge
we rot from within.

I eat you like an apple.

ONION APOLOGY

I'm sorry that you make us all cry
when we think you are so delicious.

CORNER MUSE

There are two kinds of corners
one on the inside
and one on the outside.

They may actually be
the same corner
but seen from one
arrangement
or one other.

The inside corner
is a place to put your back
when you wish to see the whole room.
Having someone in your corner
means they've got your back
means they are on your side
while
to corner someone
means to pressure them
into coercion or admission
means to confront them.

To have the corner at your back
is a powerful position

only the dunce sits facing the corner.
The outside corner
is the enemy of those afraid
of what's just around it
the outside corner is what
the curious
are sure to go around.

The world is full
of inside and outside corners
we have made
but
the spinning world
has no corners
of its own
being all
round
and globe
and sphere.

Except maybe
one inside-outside
behind the globe
of your eyes
and
the ideas
in the corner
of your mind.

EYEBROW MUSE

You are plucked hair by hair
you have a map of your follicles
tattooed on the inside of your eyelids.

You are never lost.

There is a specific order to the arch
which specifically translates your doubt
into disdain perfectly with every picking
pluck your insecurity, drown in the pin
prick of pull and you walk tall.

You think you are more wire hanger.

I terrify these cheap lines
because I can't stop knowing
how on weekends you short-sell yourself
and how that costs and costs and costs.

Now that we are older
we fear our children are our mirrors.

One day she'll meet your tweezers.

EYEBROW APOLOGY

I'm sorry I think that all the greatest muses
have unibrows with lashes which impersonate
a Water Willy and maybe continue
their outgrowth all the way around the eye
making some kind of people-owl hybrid
and that the greatest muses
don't fuss over their hair
or own a brush.

I'm sorry you
try to comb everyone over
and pull them out of their follicles
like it was a religion.

I'm sorry for
whoever plucked you first
and taught you annoyance, pain
absence, perfection was what love was.

I'm sorry the bathroom sink
has to be cleaned everyday
to cover up
the loose hairs, the evidence
of how you beat yourself up.

APPLICATION FOR A NEW MUSE

Must be willing
to be utterly destroyed
after
tearing down
every wall
and
infiltrating
our shared space
so completely
we call ourselves twins
we call ourselves one.

Must be willing to go deeper still.

Must be a reader
no exceptions
no excuses
I mean must legitimately
be obsessed with
and nurtured by
books
preferably sleeps
with
one under your pillow.

Must enjoy secretly watching me
secretly spraying your perfume
into a wad of tissue paper
which I stuff into
my pocket
so
I
can smell you
later
alone.

Must be low-key enchanting
in the way where
your eyes dart after
the first bat
of the night
and dark winds
catch your hair
on the porch step
and when you
share
your two cents
we buy
all the time in the world.

Must be bewitched
with what I create
because you get

that there's really
nothing else
that gets my panties wet
in that
needs to be wrung out
kind of way.

Must have friends
a community
a watering hole
fire pit
must be willing
to kayak down
the Missouri river
by moonlight
with a thunderstorm
on the horizon.

Mustn't be afraid of the dirt of the water.

Must be able to hold my gaze
be silent
and know when to speak again.

OCEAN MUSE

Your waves a silent inhale
and sharp rush of exhale
I breathe the rhythm of you
old women worship
at the tongue shore of you
and are for once
quiet
their bodies
soaked in sun
the sun that is
your greatest lover
and releases you
from gravity
airborne
it's always been you
mother
salt
tear
womb
tear
I worship at your body
your deep protean
your insistence
your persistence

perpetual ocean
the pull and push
of your body
against itself
even
you want to return
to yourself as I long to return
what is longing
the smooth broken tiles
of shipwrecks
remnants of porcelain
finery, green and blue
and clear glass
sand's cousin, silky now
washed ashore
next to the black sand
and fossil coral crust
and rocks with moss lichen
something green and nourished
by sun salt ocean
sea whose name means
back and forth
rocking waters
high and low tide
ocean who would be still
if not for her muse
moon
she longs for crater, impact

as I long for her inner deep
our menage a trois
on the sand
the ocean is too big
to reach the moon
and though I reach both
solomente, alone
sometime long ago
when that first small creature
pulled itself from tide and lagoon
out of the electrolytic soup
it must have somewhere
been answering the ocean's
need to reach the moon
I am your conduit, mother
I am your vehicle, mother
I am your child, dutiful
and reverent
wear me down
wear the rough edges of me down
in the relentless pushing pulling
of your abrasive waters
turn me from this edged failing
into the softness of small sand
so I can in turn wear smooth
the stones, the land
give me life, ocean
give me posterity, sea

you my ancestor and heredity
you polisher
perpetual ocean
endless autoclave of cleansing
you make each of us pristine, muse
transform me from burnished
to burnisher, take me back
within in
I never left you
my soul
I answered the high tide
of my longing and found
you again and again
I break my longing tide
against you in invocation
perpetual ocean
giver of life
source of life
I sacrifice my hard edges
my wounds to your healing pain
I drink you in
I fade away

PICKLE MUSE

I think
you are thinly sliced
and mostly made of water
and vinegar
that
you are a garnish
decorative
and
never the main course.

I love you still.

I sneak you in the afternoon
Gherkin
Bread & Butter
the whole Kosher thing
on the sunny deck
with puppy
dripping brine
and slopping the juice
on my chin.

I pretend you are
a five course meal.

PICKLE APOLOGY

I'm sorry I
loosened the lid
and let the air in
when
you were fermenting
all alone so well
sediment
your salt with green
sliced fresh grown earth
sprouted up and cut up
and preserved.

Inside you are thin.
Closed you are untouchable.

Open,
you get eaten whole.

ROOT MUSE

roots keep the tree uprigth
dig into the clay and water
roots shape the organic pottery
of the earth and dig
into the ever darker deep
to anchor
the outburst of the sapling
and the roots connect
together the forest
but also hold tight
the hill and the mountain
and hold at bay
erosion

a beet root is hard and red

you root the surface of me
and dig me up
you who are so curious
about the dirt of me
and what's underneath
and how far I can grow up

you root for me

and cheer me on
you who believe in the race
and game of me
and watch compellingly
from the sidelines

a beet root is hard and red
and sweet and round

one's roots are
the source of name
a hereditary shape
of ears which listen
the blue of an eye
wake next to me
           (every morning
           please?
           every dawn?)

root family, kindred, twin
you are at the bottom of me
you are what has made me
precisely flower fruit dew
you are what tendrils and grips
and what holds me in and up
you are what colors my lips

a beet root is hard and red

and sweet and round
and stains everything
which it touches

our fingers crisp
our roots connect
our beet red
heart swell
embrace
our bodies grown into
one another until
you and I
don't exist
only we

ROOT APOLOGY

I'm sorry I kept putting
you in different pots
trapping you in plastic
overwatering or forgetting
and I'm sorry I let the sun scorch you
I'm lucky you're so strong

PARASITIC WASP MUSE

Sleek bug eyed
cinched so tight
your pregnant disdain
is a puncture wound.

Just look at those legs, that waist
while your back end jabs me full
of your nasty little eggs
you have spine-like features
but you are not brave
ovipositor your tongue
mesmerizes me
leaves me paralyzed
because you need
to fill me up so you can live on.

Oh you stuff me up so good
before you move on
a story we both seem to know
how single mothers
teeming with progeny
squirming larvae
eat us whole
so slowly

And your small, vile spawn
emerge
more Apocrita
more plain brown parasitic wasps
single veined and six legged
small, vile things like their mother.

I live until the last
of me
is squandered
exhausted
consumed.

PARASITIC WASP APOLOGY

I'm sorry it
took me so long
to buy bug spray

& that
it
works
so
well.

CAR WRECK MUSE

That everyone is crawling around you
is not proof you are loved
but that everyone is fascinated by carnage.

I saw the red lights of brake lights
dominoed for miles in front of me.
You are proud to be so profound.
I admitted that I'd be late
that I'd do the stop and go
which meant the gawking at you:
crumpled, smoking, wrecked.

It's true I felt a little sick
but also, sickly drawn to witness
a little destruction
a happenstance cruelty
the spattergurglecrack of blood
flung across the highway
thinking of how if I'd left
a moment sooner
this near miss
might have been my collision.

I count my blessings

because there you are strung out
on the fast lane of the interstate.
You are a death sentence of leaking fluids
with two bent frames, windshields
with concentric fractures
two traumatic brain injuries
a red carpet of rubber tire tracks
leading to the main event
of your tangled and mangled
your body damage. Too bad
you are always taking
someone down with you.

Everyone is slowed down
sirens ricochet.
We're all down
to one lane
you, left
we, right
moving so slowly
slow enough to see
your bleeding tantrum.

Still, I have this sneaking suspicion
I feel sick with suspecting
how you yanked the wheel left
just to see what would happen.

SHAKER MUSE

I am the tchotchke you bought at the gift shop
in the Pittsburgh airport (to prove you had been there)
as if a snowglobe was evidence you'd seen it all.

I am the plastic town nestled close to itself
(& utterly self-contained) united by a blanket
of white glitter which is the dust of my feelings
settled in the liquid chamber of my heart.

You are the shaker which comes along
and grabs me by the glass (with both hands)
and disrupts my peaceful covering
with abrupt back & forth, back & forth & forth.

Your force sends all my plastic snowflakes
into the wet atmosphere of my containment
with the immense full moon of your distorted eye
of your newly looming face and the fisheye of teeth
(curving bared and clownish), an uncanny smile
the distortion through my dome is my best look at you.

You buy me so you own me.
I'm placed in a dark carry-on which you carry on
while you carry on with all your other dolls and trinkets

and I'm defined by a constant jostling
boarding against your hip, in the overhead
compartment: take-off, landing,
taxi home to children
(who like you, are also shakers).

Each of you watch the parts of me dance
in the whirlwind you make with your upheavals.

You set me down before the dust settles.

SHAKER APOLOGY

I'm sorry
it never crossed your mind
to imagine yourself
a part
of
my
globe.

SUBURBAN MUSE

You have a nice, clean yard
you have a steady job with decent benefits
you have a 401k, you live far enough away
you don't see factories or industry or waste
        no stacks of old railroad ties
        no dead car graveyards
        no slapdash corrugated metal
        no dilapidated buildings
        no mangy free-range dogs
        no houses with roof holes
        no oil tankers by the side of the road
        no cranes, no bulldozers loitering.

You have nice, green grass
you have a fenced yard in a gated community
you have a labradoodle named Mickey
you have a full refrigerator and pantry
        with lunchables
        with beef jerky
        with little Debbie
        with plenty of dusty cans
you have a land line you never answer
you have a TV in every room
you have 2 weeks paid vacation

you go to Florida and a beachside resort
        with Mimosas
        with Starbucks
        with Applebees
        with dolphin show at 2 pm
you go bowling every February
you have a sand volleyball league
you love groupon and tell everyone
you know where to buy the right cake
you throw the best bachelorette party
you get titillated by coming to the city
you think it means you get to be bad for a night.

The city has back alleyways covered in broken glass
the city has hand to mouth and is still hungry
the city has pavement, metal, curb and rubber
the city has sirens which means something went down
the city has people one on top of the next
the city has a culture of the night
the city has 3 am until dawn
the city has homeless camps in the woods
the city has homeless camps under the overpass
the city has pee in the street
the city has brutality
the city has poverty.

Yet, it's you, Muse of the Mall
you who have fear of dense streets

you are afraid of the close packed city
    while we celebrate a bad day
    while we drink till we go to work again
    while we cross the train tracks
    while we sneak down to the river
    while we meet sunrise in the crossroads
    the city and her fearless citizens.

SUBURBAN APOLOGY

Don't worry
not everyone is built for greatness.

DRAGON HOARD MUSE

You accessorize with wild abandon
like a cat scared up a tree by a feral dog
you leap to ring, bracelet, tiara, anklet
a chain and lock necklace you don't have keys for
an armband of actual barbed wire
a first aid kit for a purse
yet another hot or stable or big-dicked
disposable relationship
and most recently, a puppy
I mean a real 5 star movie dog
with a heart shaped spot and 3 legs.

You cast off thousands of insignificant oysters
for the pearls at your throat. The high strung vintage glam
laid over so many layers of foundation and powder
on your aging and worrisome, broken out breast
neck, your face; you cover your tracks with such panache.

Even your entire house is an adornment
for your generous anxiety.
The carefully placed every detail designed
to generate directed conversations about
the impossibility of things being different.
Every painting is perfectly level
the floors are waxed with panicked fury

clean as a whistle, you say, more often than not.
The dog is neatly asleep in the kennel, you say
though we hear him whine at the door.

Secretly, you fashion fine linens and shit
where you sleep. But at dinner, everyone laughs
while you wax traumatic on the quirky cute sickness
and slickness between your head and your thighs.

But your crown jewel, the pièce de ré·sis·tance
the singular totem we all know you by
is the prismatic diamond of your illness.
You wear the whining incantation
of a chronic aching headspace like a caul
decorated with a patterned chattering pains
to generate our obligatory and helpful reactions
endless attention, gentle condolences
the constancy of leaping to your rescue
you damsel, you Rapunzel, you sleeping beauty
you are the protagonist of every episode
in classic soap-opera, haute drame style.

The bell ring of your displaced disdain
chimes against the silver tea service
and luminous chandelier as you sing out
I just don't know ever why I keep sabotaging myself
and nervously spin the ruby rings and bangles
from wrist to elbow and all twitter and giggle

while tossing back mounds of perfectly conditioned hair.

Send the butler to shut that incessant barking up.
Click your couture heels under lace petticoats
whip the 18th century brocade Japanese fan
an anxious reflection of how your heart
is racing with all this exposure.

I won't mention your accessory of choice.

But do lift high that Waterford chalice of vintage port
and toast to high time for new wallpaper and chairs
a whole new look, in fact.

You paint yourself into a corner with such pride.
Hire yourself a new interior decorator to adorn you
in the latest craze and surround you
with the most desirable passing fashion
have them paint the mirrors with what you'd like to see.

The puppy keeps barking in the background.
Your dress is torn by his baby teeth.
You use the chain to stake him in the backyard.

For so many years to come
when he sees you he bares his teeth.

Well, it's true that you get the dog you deserve.

DRAGON HOARD APOLOGY

I'm sorry
I didn't see
that you wouldn't
share the gold coin
or keep
your forked word
I'm sorry
I didn't realize
until it was too late
that all I needed to know
about your breathing fire
i learned the day I saw
your dog bite your hand
as you fed him.

DREAM MUSE

in the small of my back
is a pain where I slept
too long
because
I fell asleep
thinking of you
next to me
my head over your
heartbeat
your hand on my cheek
drifting away
from the everyday
impossibilities
and the pain
of old houses
and the songs
once sang fade away
under closed eyes
and holding you close
and being held
by you
I slept too well
not wanting to wake up
without you

AGORAPHOBIA MUSE

Loving you is like trying to see
the horizon from the other side
of an infinite speeding train

there's this wall of metal gray
machine red, matte black
and a tiny sliver of blue peeking
flirting bright as a dream

but to go to you
to chase the horizon
you have to get run over
by the freight train.

AGORAPHOBIA APOLOGY

I'm sorry it feels like you are putting
your life on the line every time
you move an inch.

CRUTCH MUSE

If you use a crutch forever
it's because you are disabled
but I was only hurt.

You need someone perpetually injured
so you can feel useful
you wouldn't let me heal or run or fly
because you love a limp
a careful timid holding of the rails.

I promise there are plenty
of broken legs out there for you
maybe you'll luck out and find a club foot
or backwards knee, something congenital
you're hoping for cerebral palsy
with early onset juvenile arthritis
and vertigo, someone who falls a lot.

I know you kept pushing me down
so I'd stay
giving me a sprained ankle here
and a twisted knee there.

I know you hoped for another break.

And when I needed you, you were beautiful
you, who lovingly lifted me to the bath
and helped me struggle along
so slowly anyone could keep up
but I saw the side eye of jealousy
you sneered at my running shoes
my catamaran, my parachute
my library card, you hid them away
under the guise of helping me clean up.

.

CRUTCH APOLOGY

I'm sorry
for not walking away
after I stopped
needing you
I'm sorry
for using you
like you were a man
who could stand on his own two feet.

NOSTALGIA MUSE

I'm keeping a broken pocketwatch
two stopwatches and a clock that runs
but drags about a minute an hour
and makes me hopeful I can turn back time
even though I can't

I'm keeping seven scarves I'll never wear
because we used to hang them on our walls
and one scarf I bought myself later
because it has the ghost of the Colosseum
on it and in it and I don't want to forget
that tragedies get celebrated sometimes

I'm keeping the plastic dime machine polar bear
from the grocery store for which you
gave me the dime and now every time I see a dime
to this day I think of you and feel like it's good luck
even after everything fell apart and it's true
I keep all those dimes

Of course there are some odd number of books
you wanted me to read and I didn't
the vintage blender and my 14-eyelet oxblood
matching boots and the cast iron skillet

and the fancy can opener you bought me
at the hardware store with a lifelong guarantee
and like so many other things
the receipt has lost the ink which proved we owned it

I'm keeping your brother's sweatpants
and your gray knit sweater Kelsey wore
and I'm not going to break into your house
or steal and/or destroy all the things of mine
you kept or maybe I gave you
I'm not going to egg your car
because that would be ridiculous

I'm keeping my mouth shut about everything
because the only thing really left
is a promise I made to myself
to not take any more anything from you

NOSTALGIA APOLOGY

I'm sorry the best we could keep
were trinkets which remind us
of what we couldn't keep.

HOKEY POKEY MUSE

I haven't your knack
for the easy uselessness
I haven't your quack
quack quacking
duck duck goosing
and dodge
ball-games and board games
or how you bend over
backwards to limbo
you are so inbetween
how your right arm in
and then right arm out
as if you were born to it
and jigsaw about as though
your piece fit every empty slot
all hokey pokey and London bridges
you are always sent over red rover
you turn yourself around
and falling down
you are the blackjack dealer
of reindeer games and I
am red nose
last chose
benchwarmer.

THE MUSE IS PRESENT

It's ok to let each other go
because we are never really gone
I can't look at the world without seeing you in it.

Today, you were the first green sprig in February
destined to be the little daffodils and I laughed
with you because of how you always push through.
Today, you were me, climbing up the steep coast
of the dry creek with two books in hand
and I didn't fall because you always
are so sure of where you stand.
And then you were the prickly green briar
I grabbed a handful of inadvertently
to pull myself up over the fallen tree
because of how you bite when I'm in need.

Now, you are the thorns I pull from my palm.
Now, you are the rustle of the winds lifting
the leaves and hustling them away.
Now you are the slip of blue sky framing
tree branches light with new bud.
Because you are the pain and struggle of creation
because you are the unearthing of a new life
because you are the unreachable horizon
I am forever reaching towards.

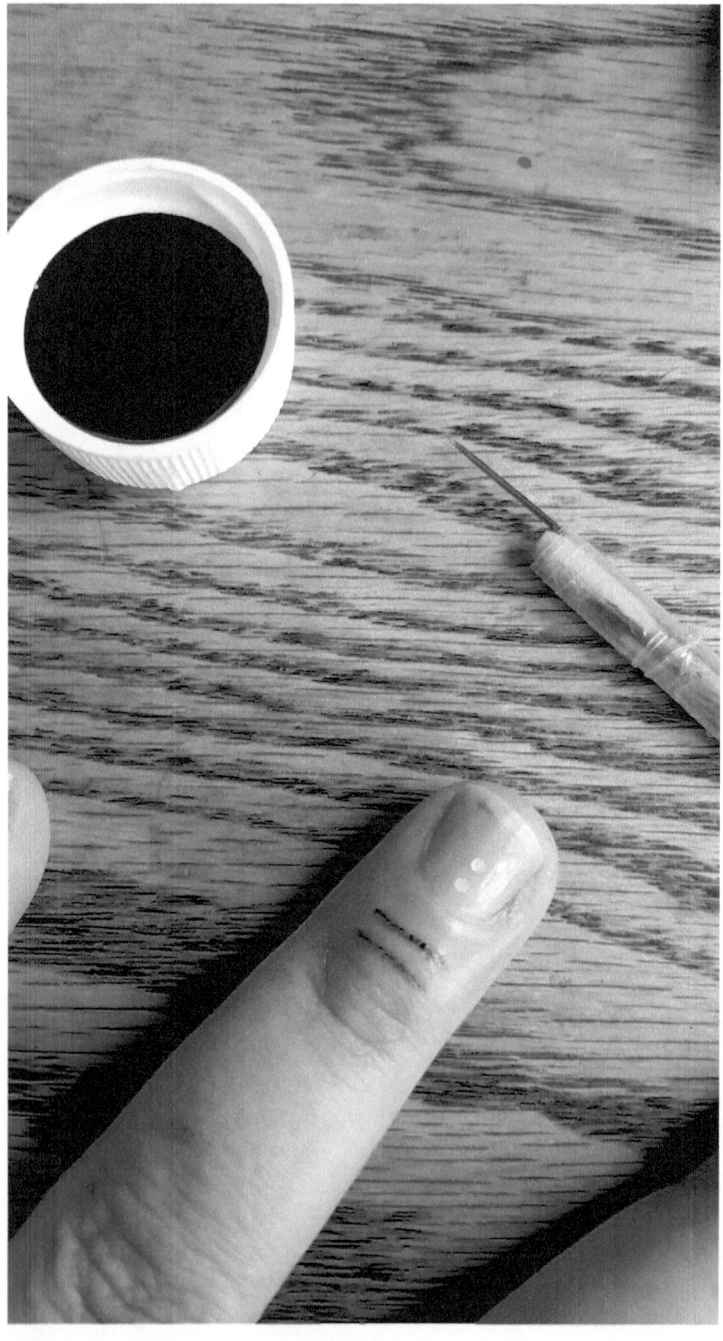

www.ingramcontent.com/pod-product-compliance
Lightning Source LLC
Chambersburg PA
CBHW021453080526
44588CB00009B/827